HE THAT IS AWAKE
LIGHTS UP FROM SLEEPING.
—HERAKLEITOS

The Behavior of Titans
by Thomas Merton

A NEW DIRECTIONS BOOK

New Directions Books are published at
Norfolk, Conn. by James Laughlin
New York office: 333 Sixth Avenue, New York 14

FOR
LAURENS
VAN DER POST

Ex Parte Ordinis

NIHIL OBSTAT

    Frater M. Gabriel O'Connell, O.C.S.O.
    Frater M. Paul Bourne, O.C.S.O.
    Frater M. Thomas Aquinas Porter, O.C.S.O.

IMPRIMI POTEST

    Frater M. Gabriel Sortais, O.C.S.O.
    Abbas Generalis

The Contents

◆ PART ONE
The Behavior of Titans

◆ 1

A Note: Two Faces of Prometheus

ERASMUS once discussed with Colet and other divines the nature of Cain's sin: not the murder of Abel but his *first* sin. Their conclusions are no longer interesting or important. The only reason I allude to the discussion is that the Cain of Erasmus turned out to be Prometheus in a fable that tells us much about the mentality of the Renaissance—and about our own.

Cain, says Erasmus, had often heard his parents speak of the wonderful vegetation of Paradise, where the "ears of corn were as high as the alders," and he persuaded the angel at the gate to bring him a few seeds from inside the garden. He planted them and succeeded admirably as a farmer, but this drew down upon him the wrath of the Almighty. His sacrifices were no longer acceptable.

It is curiously significant that modern and "progressive" man should consider himself somehow called upon to vindicate Cain, and that in doing so he should identify Cain with the fire-bearing Titan whom he has been pleased to make the symbol of his own technological genius and of his cosmic aspirations.

11

But what is equally significant is the confusion of the two opposite interpretations of Prometheus: the version of Hesiod, in which Prometheus is a villain, and the version of Aeschylus in which he is the hero. The difference between these two versions lies of course in the different attitude toward the implacable father figure: Zeus.

Hesiod represents and approves the Olympian order, where Zeus reigns in absolute power over the subversive and dethroned gods of archaic Greece. Zeus is the god of the invading Achaians who destroyed the matriarchal and tribal society of primitive Greece, the society of the Earth Mother, of Demeter, of Hera and Athene. Prometheus, the son of Earth and of Ocean is a threat to the static order established by Zeus, the order in which no bird may chirp and no flower may look at the sun without the permission of the jealous Father. Zeus is the master of life rather than its giver. He tolerates man and man's world, but only barely.

According to Hesiod, when Prometheus *stole* the fire for men (there was no other way in which he could get fire away from Zeus) Zeus revenged himself on Prometheus in the way we well know with the added detail that he drives a stake through his heart. But Zeus is also revenged upon mankind: how? By sending woman.

Strange, ponderous fantasy of an aggressively male society! Woman comes from Zeus as a *punishment*, for in her "everything is good but her heart."

Woman, the culminating penance in a life of labor and sorrow!

In the world picture of Hesiod, though it is beautiful, primitive, full of Hellenic clarity, we find this darkness, this oppressive and guilty view that life and love are some- how a punishment. That nothing can ever be really good in it. That life is slavery and sorrow because of Zeus, and because Prometheus has resisted Zeus. That therefore life is nothing but a wheel upon which man is broken like a slave. . . .

Epimetheus, the brother of Prometheus, receives woman as a gift from Zeus and does not wake up to the nature of the gift until it is too late. Then he remembers what Prometheus had told him: *never accept any gift from the gods.*

Hesiod is a great poet and yet to me this view of life is utterly horrible. I hate it and I reject it with everything in my being. All the more because it is, I believe, implicit in the atheism of the world into which I was born and out of which, by Christ's grace and the gift of God, I have been reborn.

The *Prometheus Bound* of Aeschylus is one of the most heart-rending, pure and sacred of tragedies. I know of none that strikes so deep into the roots of man, the root where man is able to live in the mystery of God.

The Prometheus of Aeschylus is the exact opposite of the Prometheus of Hesiod. Between Prometheus and the Earth Mother and Ocean rises the figure of a usurper. For in Aeschylus it is Zeus, not Prometheus, who is the usurper. It is Zeus, not Prometheus, who is sick with *hubris*. True, Prometheus is driven by desperation beyond the wise limits which the Greek mind recognized so well. But his rebellion is the rebellion of life against inertia, of mercy and love against tyranny, of humanity against cruelty and arbitrary violence. And he calls upon the feminine, the wordless, the timelessly moving elements to witness his sufferings. Earth hears him.

14

In the end of the tragedy (which is only the first of a trilogy, two plays of which have been lost) Earth promises her son a deliverer. Herakles will come and break his brother's chains. Zeus will be mollified. His mind will change, and he will see things in a new light. The struggling gods will be reconciled, and the reconciliation will be the victory of Prometheus but also the victory of Earth, that is to say of mercy, of humanity, of innocence, of trust.

Once more it will be possible for men to receive gifts from heaven. It will be possible and right to wait for gifts, to depend on them. To use them to build, innocently, a better world.

The two faces of Prometheus represent two attitudes toward life, one positive, the other negative. It is significant that the Renaissance, in choosing between the two, selected the negative. It is against this negative choice that my Prometheus is written. My meditation is a rejection of the negative, modern myth of Prometheus. It is a return to the archaic, Aeschylean and positive aspect of Prometheus, which is, at the same time, to my mind, deeply and implicity Christian.

The Prometheus of Hesiod is Cain. The Promethus of Aeschylus is Christ on the Cross.

In my meditation I have started from Hesiod's view in order to argue against it.

Prometheus: A Meditation

1. The small gods men have made for themselves are jealous fathers, only a little greater than their sons, only a little stronger, only a little wiser. Immortal fathers, afraid of their mortal children, they are unjustly protected by a too fortunate immortality. To fight with them requires at once heroism and despair. The man who does not know the Living God is condemned, by his own gods, to this despair: because, knowing that he has made his own gods, he cannot help hoping that he will be able to overthrow them. Alas, he realizes too late that he has made them immortal. They must eventually devour him.

15

2. The Promethean instinct is as deep as man's weakness: that is to say, it is almost infinite. Promethean despair is the cry that rises out of the abyss of man's nothingness — the inarticulate expression of the terror man cannot face, the terror of having to be someone, of having to be himself. That is to say, his terror of facing and fully realizing his divine sonship, in Christ, and in the Spirit of Fire Who is given us from heaven. The fire Prometheus thought he had to steal from the gods is his own identity in God, the affirmation and vindication of his own being as a sanctified creature in the image of God. The fire Prometheus thought he had to steal was his own spiritual freedom. In the eyes of Prometheus to be himself was to be guilty. The exercise of liberty was a crime, an attack upon the gods which he had made (the gods to whom he had given all that was good in himself, so that in order to have all that he had, it was necessary to steal it back from them).

3. Prometheus knows — for his nature tells him this — that he must become a person. Yet he feels that he can only do this by an exploit, a *tour-de-force*. And the exploit itself is doomed to failure. Condemned by his very nature to face this gesture and this crime, he feels drawn, by his very nature itself, to extinction. The fire attracts him more than he can believe possible, because it is in reality his own. But he hates himself for desiring what he has given to his gods, and punishes himself before he can take it back from them. Then he becomes his own vulture, and is satisfied at last. In consuming himself, he finds realization. (Secretly he tells himself: "I have won fire for other men, I have sacrificed myself for others." But in reality he has won nothing for anybody. He has suffered the loss of his own soul, but he has not gained the whole world, or even a small part of it. He has gained nothing.)

4. Guilty, frustrated, rebellious, fear-ridden, Prometheus seeks to assert himself

and fails. His mysticism enables him to glory in defeat. For since Prometheus cannot conceive of a true victory, his own triumph is to let the vulture devour his liver: he will be a martyr and a victim, because the gods he has created in his own image represent his own tyrannical demands upon himself. There is only one issue in his struggle with them: glorious defiance in a luxury of despair.

To struggle with the gods seems great, indeed, to those who do not know the Living God. They do not know that He is on our side against false gods and defeat is not permissible. One who loves Christ is not allowed to be Prometheus. He is not allowed to fail. He must *keep* the fire that is given him from heaven. And he must assert that the fire is *his*. He must maintain his rights against all the false gods who hold that it was stolen.

5. Guilt was the precious gift of the false gods to Prometheus, a gift that made all this waste possible. Not knowing that the fire was his for the asking, a gift of the true God,

the Living God, not knowing that fire was something God did not need for Himself (since He had made it expressly for man) Prometheus felt he was obliged to steal what he could not do without. And why? Because he knew no god that would be willing to give it to him for nothing. He could not conceive of such a god, because if he himself had been god, he would have needed fire for himself and would never have shared it with another. He knew no god that was not an enemy, because the gods he knew were only a little stronger than himself, and needed fire as badly as he needed it. In order to exist at all, they had to dominate him and feed on him and ruin him (for if he himself had been a god, he knew he would have had to live on what was weaker than himself).

Thus the gods Prometheus knew were weak, because he himself was weak. Yet they were a little stronger than he was, strong enough to chain him to Caucasus. (He had that much strength left in himself, after creating his gods: he was strong enough to consume himself for all eternity in punishment for having desired their fire. In fact, he destroyed himself forever that they might live. For this reason idolatry was, and is, the fundamental sin.)

6. A man must make the best of whatever gods he has. Prometheus had to have weak gods because he was his own god, and no man admits that he is his own god. But he subjects himself to his own weakness, conceived as a god, and prefers it to the strength of the Living God. If Prometheus had known the strong God, and not worshiped weak gods, things would have been different. The guilt Prometheus felt from the beginning was more necessary for his gods than for himself. If he had not been guilty, such gods would not have been able to exist. Without guilt he could not have conceived them, and since they only existed in his own mind he had to be guilty in order to think of them at all. His guilt, then, was a secret expression of

love. It was his homage of love and trust. By his guilt he bore witness to his little household gods, his fire-hoarders. By stealing their fire he confessed that he loved them and believed in their falsity more than he loved the Living God and more than he believed in His truth. It was then a supreme act of homage on his part to open his heart to his unreal gods, and steal from them that fire which, in reality, was his own. Surely, he had given them everything, in order to show how much he preferred their nothingness to the Living God and even to himself!

7. No one was ever less like Prometheus on Caucasus, than Christ on His Cross. For Prometheus thought he had to ascend into heaven to steal what God had already decreed to give him. But Christ, Who had in Himself all the riches of God and all the poverty of Prometheus, came down with the fire Prometheus needed, hidden in His Heart. And He had Himself put to death next to the thief Prometheus in order to show him that in

reality God cannot seek to keep anything good to Himself alone.

22

Far from killing the man who seeks the divine fire, the Living God will Himself pass through death in order that man may have what is destined for him.

If Christ has died and risen from the dead and poured out upon us the fire of His Holy Spirit, why do we imagine that our desire for life is a Promethean desire, doomed to punishment?

Why do we act as if our longing to "see good days" were something God did not desire, when He Himself told us to seek them? Why do we reproach ourselves for desiring victory? Why do we pride ourselves on our defeats, and glory in despair?

Because we think our life is important to ourselves alone, and do not know that our life is more important to the Living God than it is to our own selves.

Because we think our happiness is for ourselves alone, and do not realize that it is also His happiness.

Because we think our sorrows are for ourselves alone, and do not believe that they are much more than that: they are His sorrows.

There is nothing we can steal from Him at all, because before we can think of stealing it, it has already been given.

Atlas and the Fat Man

On the last day of a rough but fortunate voyage, near the farthest end of the known world, I found my way to the shores of a sentient mountain.

There stood the high African rock in the shadow of lucky rain: a serious black crag, at the tip of the land mass, with a cloud balanced on its shoulder.

O high silent man of lava, with feet in the green surf, watching the stream of days and years!

We saw the clouds drift by the face of that tame god, and held our peace. We placed our feet on the hot sands as the ship was beached on the edge of night and of summer.

This was Atlas at his lonely work! I never thought I would have seen his face!

His head was hidden in sky. His eyes were staring darkness. His thoughts were full of inscrutable waters. His heart was safe at the bottom of the green ocean. His spirit stood silent and awake in the center of the world.

He held everything in massive silence. In one deep thought without words he kept the continents from drifting apart. The seas obeyed not his eyes, not his words, but the beating of his heart.

His only utterance was one weak light in a lighthouse. Small sharp words, no commentary on the pure mystery of night, they left the mystery alone: touched it and left it alone.

From time to time he spoke (but only to the distance) with the short bass clangor of a bell. The neutral note was uttered, and said nothing.

Yet it was this dim bell in the heavens that

moved the weather and changed the seasons.

A new summer grew upon the ocean, before our eyes, closely followed by autumn, then winter.

The waves moved by with white hair. Time rode the secret waves, commanded only by Atlas and by his bell. There were ages passing by as we watched. Birds skimmed the white-haired ages. Young birds kept the morning young. The silence of this unvisited shore embraced the beginning of history and its end.

We made believe that it was five o'clock. We made believe that it was six o'clock. We made believe that it was midnight. Atlas must have deigned to smile on our efforts, since it was now dark. His eyes gave hope to the tumbling ocean. Once again, rain began to fall.

*   *   *

When it is evening, when night begins to darken, when rain is warm in the summer darkness and rumors come up from the

woods and from the banks of rivers, then
shores and forests sound around you with a
wordless solicitude of mothers. It is then
that flowering palms enchant the night with
their sweet smell. Flowers sleep. Thoughts
become simple. Words cease. The hollows of
the mind fill with dreams as with water.

In the sacred moment between sleeping and
staying awake, Atlas speaks to the night as to
a woman. He speaks freely to the night he
loves, thinking no one is at hand.

He speaks, of his heart at the bottom of the
ocean. He speaks of his spirit at the center of
the world. He speaks of fires that night, and
woman, do not understand. Green fires that
are extinguished by intelligence, that night
and woman possess. Golden fires of spirit
that are in the damp warm rocky roots of the
earth. White fires that are clear outside of
earth and sky which night and woman cannot reach. And waters that are common to
night and to woman and to Atlas, ruled by a
bell in the moon and by a bell in the sun.

28 Atlas puts out all those fires with his one bell, and looks at nothing. This is the work that supports the activity of seasons: Atlas looking at nothing.

"How lonely is my life as a mountain on the shore of ocean with my heart at the bottom of the sea and my spirit at the center of the earth where no one can speak to me. I ring my bell and nobody listens. All I do is look at nothing and change the seasons and hold up the sky and save the world.

"No one will come near to one so tall, no one will befriend one so strong as I, and I am forgotten forever. It is right that I be forgotten, for if I were not forgotten where would be my vigilance, and if I were not vigilant where would be the world? And if night and woman could understand my thoughts, where would be my strength? My thoughts would draw up my spirit from the center of the earth and the whole world would fall into emptiness.

"My stability is without fault because I have no connections. I have not viewed mankind for ages. Yet I have not slept, thinking of man and his troubles, which are not alleviated by the change of seasons. I wish well to mankind. I give man more seasons and pray that he be not left to himself. I want him not to see my far lights upon the ocean (this is impossible) or hear my dim bell in the heavens (this is not expedient). But I want him to rest at peace under a safe sky knowing that I am here with my lights and my bell and that the ends of the world are watched by an overseer and the seas taken care of.

"I do not tire easily, for this is the work I am used to. Though it is child's play, sometimes I hate it. I bear with loneliness for the sake of man. Yet to be constantly forgotten is more than I can abide.

"Thus I intend not only to watch, but to move watching, and I shall begin by moving the theaters."

At this there was a stir in all the distant cities of the world and the continents heaved up and down like the trays of a scale, as all the great countries were suddenly weighed by Atlas in the middle of the night: the lands of Europe and the lands of Asia were weighed in the hands of a tall hidden power, and knew nothing of it. The shores of America waited in the mist to be weighed in the same balance. It was Atlas, the guardian of nights and seas moving and watching.

We expected movement only after it had already begun and we looked for power when the strong were already overthrown. We saw the dance begin secretly in genteel houses, under the kitchen oilcloth and leap to the tops of the most public monuments. Some buildings woke and walked downhill and would not stop until they came to water. Churches and banks begged pardon as they slipped and fell. People in the unsafe doors set out for earth that escaped them, and trod too late on streets that hurried away. It was more than most men could afford but far more than they could avoid. It was a lame evening. No taxi would take any man to the right place.

This was what happened everywhere when the movement began. The title of the earthquake was "Atlas watches every evening."

* * *

Then up jumped a great fatman in one of the stadiums. He thought that he was god and that he could stop everything from moving. He thought that since he could, he had to. He cried out loud. He swore at the top of his voice. He fired off a gun and made the people listen. He roared and he boasted and made himself known. He blew back into the wind and stamped on the rolling earth and swore up and down he could make it all stop with his invention. He got up in the teeth of the storm and made a loud speech which everybody heard. And the first thing he said was this:

"If anything moves, I am the one to move it: and if anything stops, I am the one to stop it. If anything shakes I am the one to shake it, and not one thing is going to budge unless pushed."

At that moment everything stopped. No one had heard the dim bell at the edge of the sea (which Atlas had struck, in his dream, at this very moment). No one saw the lights in the dark at the edge of the ocean, (which had gone on and off with a passing memory in that far place). No one thought of anything, the fatman had all their attention.

*　　*　　*

Now this fatman had been brought up on oats and meat and his name was secret. His father was a grocer and his mother was a butcher. His father was a tailor and his mother ran a train. His father was a brewer and his mother was a general in the army. He had been born with leather hands and a clockwork mind in order to make a lot of money. He hated the country and loved stadiums: a perfect, civilized man! His number was six hundred and sixty-six and he worked hard building up the stadium Atlas had destroyed.

All the people brought him money and played music to him because he was rich. And the music was so loud no one heard the bell ring again. Once again the houses began to tremble.

No one looked at anything, but fixed their eyes only on the fatman in his rage. No one heard Atlas far off thinking in the smoke. All they knew was that the city began to fall again and the fatman roared in the tumble-down theaters: "If I had my way there would be RAIN." He held up his hands and had his way. Rain came down as sudden as a black mountain. The clock struck ten. The world stopped moving. Everyone attributed this to the fatman whose name was secret.

Then in the holes of the broken city the sergeants smiled safe and guns became a thing of the present. Gas was mercy then to many a Jew mother and a quick end came to more than a few as a gift of the popular state. "Here comes a chemical death, with the smile of the public Father. You shall be cheaply made extinct as a present from economy, and we will save your hair and teeth. Cyanide hopes are the face of a popular tomorrow, with ever more fun in the under-wears. Everybody has dollars in the home of well-run Demos, and more for cars than for Sunday. But Sunday is public also where Fatman has his office. Only a different name, that's all.

"Here comes chemical Sunday, with a smile of the Fatman's ghost father. They take the girth of the Fat Father's own gas, on top of the ancient marsh, in the name of a new culture. Toy thugs jump out of every cradle with weapons in their hands. They swing by hard and mean in the name of popularity and boy, that popularity is going to make you jump. It is already famous what they can do with guns, and more so with a piece of small invented pipe, all for the fame and benefit of the new police. Fatman, Fatman, blow us a gassy kiss from the four chimneys of your new heaven!"

From the four sides of the wind there came together in trolleys a set of delegations in the name of Dad. "Not forgetting Mom" they blowed, "we come to hail the Fatman in the name of Dad." And old Dad sat up high in the memories of the police, a nineteenth-century legend, a corncob angle measuring the west.

A piece of trueblue oldgold faked-up fortune. True
Dad is all fixed up in the mind like a piece of Real
Estate, but Mom (cries the Fatman) Mom is real **35**
heart and all soft in the easies. Mom is fat from toe
to toe, and slimmer than an ankle. Good old American
Maw is Father's boast on wedding-cake afternoon, in
the days of Coca-Cola. Maw is safe in the new car and
Paw cares for corners. The eyes of the innocent
sergeant salute Maw with pride as they draw Jewish
blood. And we will have a clean America for our
boys, clean as the toy toughs punished in rugged Lux.
Tomboy Maw is the magic of Fatman's perpetual
boast.

* * *

Then the fatman moved by intuition placed
his feet in the water and established contact
with the spirit of night and the waves
thrashed about his knees. All at once he
began to grow. He gave up meat to become
an ascetic. He drank only the most inexpen-
sive mouthwash. He dealt with woman
only by mail. He tried out his hands on the
sky and began to hold up the firmament.
He would hold up the sky and preach at the
same time, for he was suddenly religious.
He began to list all the dates of history and

to tell men another word for love and another word for death. He said he himself was the eldest child of love and death, but principally of death. At this he returned to his meat and dropped his letters and dealt with woman once again directly. He said he could also tell them another name for woman. The people took down notes of what he said next, and he told them his own real name was god.

*   *   *

We who stood far off amid the tears of the African night, we who stood with our feet on a hot land, we knew who had rung the bell and changed the weather. We knew who had sent rain. We knew which was power and which was image, which was light and which was legend. And we knew which of the two had his heart at the bottom of the ocean. We knew who watched and who moved under the theaters every time the bell rang. We listened intently to the cloud and the darkness. We lived upon distance, and leaned upon emptiness until we heard our mountain think plain in his own cloud.

"Smoke is not measured by clocks" said Atlas. "Time is not told by disasters. Years are not numbered by the wars that are in them, days are not marked on the calendar for the murders that take place on them. What is it that you are measuring, fatman? What is it that you are interpreting with your machine, meatman? What is it that you are counting, you square, serious stepson of death?

"I take my own time," said Atlas "which is the time of the sea. The sea tells its own long time, not by the moon or by the sun or by any clock. The time of the sea is infinitely various, and out of it comes all life: but only when the time of the sea is the time of the sun. Not the time of rising and setting, but the time of light itself, which has no hours.

"The sea's time is the time of long life. The jungle's time is the time of many rains. The spirit of the trees takes time out of the slow earth and the leaves are made of this earth-time turning into light. Longer life still undersea, for invisible Tritons. The long life of the earth. The life of spinning suns.

"The gods of the sea tell no time. They are busy with their own music. I Atlas improve the world with mists, evenings and colors. I have my own music of clouds, skies and centuries. I strike music from far continents. Others do not hear. They have heard nothing of this for a long time. They have heard clock and cannon, not my music. They have eaten smoke and gone down by train to the last mute home of welfare, which is the end.

"Sad is the city of the fatman, for all his industry. Snow cannot make softer the city of the fatman, which is always black in its own breath. Rain cannot wash clean the city of the mercenary, which is always gray with his own despair. Light cannot make fair their houses or wine their faces, though they swim in millions they have won. The fatman

with his inventions is propping up a fallen
heaven."

Shall we forget the periods of his earthly
mischief, not with regret? Shall we forget
the fatman and his false rain? The people in
that city shuddered and the rain ran down
their necks and the fatman struggled with
his stadium.

"Fatman" said Atlas "you are a faithless mad
son of clocks and buzzers. I do not know
what apparatus was your sire, you bastard of
two machines, born with another million.
Your mother is not the ocean, your father
has not the sun in his heart, you do not know
the smell of the earth, your blood is not your
own, it is taken from armies. A red flash
goes on and off for every thought in your
head and a buzzer announces your latest
word. I abhor the traffic that comes from
such a mad, convulsive mouth. It is the
mouth of a horde, the mouth of a system,
the mouth of a garage, the mouth of a
commission."

Atlas stopped speaking and the rain ended. The fatman raged in his place and all the people sweated under attack. Crowds expected the fatman to stand up for his honor and for the first time to move the world with his invention. Instead he only argued with himself and though he bragged he instantly called himself a liar. But in the same breath he accused Atlas of the most shameful infamies. "Atlas is responsible," he said "for doors and windows, stairs, chimneys, and every other form of evil." In attacking Atlas he ended by moving no one but himself, and this was the burden of his display:

"Thirteen is an unlucky number and there are *thirteen in this theater*." (This was his first bravery and very nearly his last, the heart of his argument. For though he said much more, he barely moved beyond this point: oh lucky thirteen!)

"Do you see," he cried, "do you see around me the thirteen beards of Victor Hugo and Karl Marx? Do you see around me the spectacles of Edison, Rockefeller, and behind me the comforting pokerfaces of Stakhanov and Patton? Do you see above my head the thirteen mustaches of Hitler and of Stalin? You who see these thirteen see me and my fathers. . . .

"Now I have fought the elements for thirteen days and nights with my invention. The elements will never be the same again. There were thirteen floods when the world was destroyed for the first time and thirteen sat together at supper in one room when very big business was done by my cousin Judas. (My cousins all prosper in business. We are not lucky in love.)

"Now that the fates are measuring more fires for the cities of men, and I myself am inventing more of them, and walls begin to shake at the work of the atheist Atlas, I stand here to defy walls, fires, earthquake and enemy. I stand here to defy Atlas. Yes I stand here in the name of clean government to defy this upsquirt downpush four-five-six

confusion of aliens. Yes I maintain this Atlas
is no longer public, and never was mechanical. Is he insured? Has he a license? Ask
him for his card, his thumbprint, and his
serial number. Has he been registered? Has
he been certified? I have been all these
things not once but thirteen times, which
is fourteen stars on my best stripe. I am the
auspicious beginning and the prosperous end,
the lucky winner and the marvelous defeat.
I am alone in the public eye on thirteen
counts. Mine is the middle of the stadium.

"I alone shall shake walls in the future. I
alone shall light thirteen fires, or more, or
less. I alone shall determine right and wrong;
establish time and season; plan day and night
as I please, and the sex and the future of
children. I alone shall spite or command sea,
wind and element. And now by God I hear
thirteen allegedly just men walking under
the oilcloth and if they don't stop
I'LL FIRE!"

* * *

Well as you might expect, the citizens came
out with bands to hail the fatman, since this
had been arranged. But the fatman by now
was lost in his own smoke. The strength
ebbed out of his invention, and his hands fell
slack; his eyes popped out and his fat began
to get away from him in all the heat he had
caused with his speech. The men in the bands
continued to perspire and blow. Their horns
would shiver till the drums fell in. There
was no rain and the fatman was smaller than
a baby. Winds were still as death; buildings
swayed for the last fall. Everyone knew the
fatman would not get out of the way in time.
Generals cried to the fatman as they left by
all windows, telling him to jump, but nobody
heard his answer.

Then Atlas stood over the world holding up
the sky like a great wall of clear ice and the
fatman saw Atlas was not his friend. The
fatman was blinded by the glare of the ice
and closed his eyes upon a world that had
been made hateful by his own folly.

44 So winter comes to the ocean and the quiet
city wears plumes of smoke upon helmets of
ice. It is a time of golden windows and of a
steel sun, a time of more bitter cruelty than
before, though the fatman is gone. For even
the just man now kills without compunction,
because it is duty to be hard and to destroy is
mercy. Justice is a myth made of numbers.
Mercy is love of system. Christmas goes by
without a sound because there are no sinners
any more, every one is just.

*　*　*

No need of feast days when everyone is just:
no one needs to be saved. No one needs to
think. No one needs to confess.

The cold saints of the new age count with
their machine the bitter, methodical sacrifices
they are making in the fatman's memory,
and stand in line before his tomb. Sacrifice
is counted in drops of blood (where blood is
still left, for many can do without it).

Minutes are counted like Aztecs walking a
man to his death with his heart out on top of

a bad pyramid: such is order and justice.
Such is the beauty of system.

So the children of scandal sit all day in the icy
windows and try in vain to shed one tear:
but in a time of justice tears are of no avail.

For the just man there is no consolation.

For the good there is no pardon.

For the holy there is no absolution.

Let no man speak of anything but Law, and
let no work support anyone but the police.

These are the saints the fatman has left us in
the kingdom of his order. . . .

Yet Titans under the sea must once again
move. When warmth comes again to the sea,
the Titans of spring shall wake. Life shall
wake underground and under sea. The fields
will laugh, the woods will be drunk with
flowers of rebellion, the night will make
every fool sing in his sleep and the morning
will make them stand up in the sun and
cover themselves with water and with light.

46 There is another kind of justice than the justice of number, which can neither forgive nor be forgiven. There is another kind of mercy than the mercy of Law which knows no absolution. There is a justice of newborn worlds which cannot be counted. There is a mercy of individual things that spring into being without reason. They are just without reason, and their mercy is without explanation. They have received rewards beyond description because they themselves refuse to be described. They are virtuous in the sight of God because their names do not identify them. Every plant that stands in the light of the sun is a saint and an outlaw. Every tree that brings forth blossoms without the command of man is powerful in the sight of God. Every star that man has not counted is a world of sanity and perfection. Every blade of grass is an angel singing in a shower of glory.

These are worlds of themselves. No man can use or destroy them. Theirs is the life

that moves without being seen and cannot
be understood. It is useless to look for what
is everywhere. It is hopeless to hope for what
cannot be gained because you already have it.
The fire of a wild white sun has eaten up the
distance between hope and despair. Dance in
this sun you tepid idiot. Wake up and dance
in the clarity of perfect contradiction.

You fool, it is life that makes you dance:
have you forgotten? Come out of the smoke,
the world is tossing in its sleep, the sun is up,
the land is bursting in the silence of dawn.
The clear bell of Atlas rings once again over
the sea and the animals come to the shore at
his feet. The gentle earth relaxes and spreads
out to embrace the strong sun. The grasses
and flowers speak their own secret names.
With his great gentle hands, Atlas opens the
clouds and birds spill back onto the land out
of Paradise.

You fool, the prisons are open. The fatman
is forgotten. The fatman was only his own
nightmare. Atlas never knew him. Atlas

48 never knew anything but the ways of the stars, of the earth and of the ocean. Atlas is a friendly mountain, with a cloud on his shoulder, watching the rising sun.

◆ ◆ PART TWO

The Guilty Bystander

◆ ◆ 1

Letter to an Innocent Bystander

If I dare, in these few words, to ask you
some direct and personal questions, it is
because I address them as much to myself
as to you. It is because I am still able to hope
that a civil exchange of ideas can take place
between two persons — that we have not
yet reached the stage where we are all her-
metically sealed, each one in the collective
arrogance and despair of his own herd. If I
seem to be in a hurry to take advantage of
the situation that still exists, it is, frankly,
because I sometimes feel it may not continue
to exist much longer. In any case, I still
believe that we are still sufficiently "persons"
to realize we have a common difficulty, and
to try to solve it together. I write this, then, **51**

in the hope that we can still save ourselves from becoming numbers.

You can easily guess that in using the term "innocent bystander" I had to examine my conscience to see whether or not I was being facetious. I do not remember if I smiled when I first thought of it, but in any case I am no longer smiling. For I do not think the question of our innocence can be a matter for jesting, and I am no longer certain that it is honorable to stand by as the helpless witness of a cataclysm, with no other hope than to die innocently and by accident, as a non-participant.

But who are "we"? We are the intellectuals who have taken for granted that we could be "bystanders" and that our quality as detached observers could preserve our innocence and relieve us of responsibility. By intellectual, I do not mean clerk, (though I might mean *clerc*). I do not mean bureaucrat. I do not mean politician. I do not mean technician. I do not mean any one whose intelligence ministers to a machine for counting, classifying, and distributing other people: who hands out to this one a higher pay check and to that one a trip (presently) to the forced labor camp. I do not mean a policeman, or a propagandist. I still dare to use the word intellectual as if it had a meaning.

So here we stand, you and I, while "they" attend to their increasingly sinister affairs, and we observe: "Well, let others mind their own business and we will mind ours." Such an attitude soon leads to another, hardly innocent, in which we may find ourselves saying: "You can't make an omelet without breaking eggs." From this it is but one step to a doctrine even more timely and more consoling: "You can't break eggs without making an omelet." If you have already got that far there is no use in reading any more of this letter.

This inspires me to ask my first dangerous question. "Although it seems to be impos-

54 sible to do anything but stand and wait, is our waiting harmless, and is it innocent? Can we afford to remain inert? Can we afford to confuse helplessness with honesty? It is true that if one is helpless, honesty requires that he admit it. But if he is helpless through his own neglect, he can hardly permit himself to be complacent in an admission of helplessness that is not, at the same time, an admission of guilt."

You will answer: "Waiting is not inertia. To be quiet and bide one's time is to resist. Passive resistance is a form of action."

That is true when one is waiting for something, and knows for what he is waiting. That is true when one is resisting, and knows why, and to what end, he is resisting, and whom he must resist. Unless our waiting implies knowledge and action, we will find ourselves waiting for our own destruction and nothing more. A witness of a crime, who just stands by and makes a mental note of the fact that he is an innocent bystander, tends by that very fact to become an accomplice.

Are we waiting for anything? Do we stand for anything? Do we know what we want?

Here we stand, in a state of diffuse irritation and doubt, while "they" fight one another for power over the whole world. It is our confusion that enables "them" to use us, and to pit us against one another, for their own purposes. Our guilt, our deep resentment, do nothing to preserve us from a shameful fate. On the contrary, our resentment is what fits us most perfectly to be "their" instruments. How can we claim that our inertia is innocent? It is the source of our guilt.

Is non-participation possible? Can complicity be avoided? You in your country and I in mine — you in your circle and I in my monastery: does the fact that we hate and resent tyranny and try to dissociate ourselves from it suffice to keep us innocent?

First, let us assume that we are clear who "they" are. When I speak of "them," you will understand that I mean those special

ones who seek power over "all the others,"
and who use us as instruments to gain power
over the others. Thus there are three groups
I am thinking of: "they," "we" and "the
others." We, the intellectuals, stand in the
middle, and we must not forget that, in the
end, everything depends on *us*.

It is therefore supremely important for us
not to yield to despair, abandon ourselves to
the "inevitable" and identity ourselves with
"them." Our duty is to refuse to believe that
their way is "inevitable." And it is equally
important for us not to set ourselves too
exclusively apart from "the others" who
depend on us, and upon whom we ourselves
also depend.

As for the powerful ones, it is our job to
recognize them even without their police,
even before the establishment of their
machinery. We must identify them wherever
"they" may appear, even though they may
rise up in the midst of ourselves, or among
"the others." We must be able to recognize

"them" by what they *are* and not rest satisfied with what is said about them, by others
or by themselves or above all by one of us!
It is already rare for an intellectual to retain
his sense of judgment when "they" change
their masks and reshuffle their labels and put
on different badges. Yet "they" are always
"they." It is to their obvious interest to pay
us to give them a new name, a false identity,
especially since, in doing so, we convince
ourselves that we have made a brilliant dis-
covery. We must not let our vanity provide
"them" with false passports.

Let us assume, at this point, that we are not
interested in their money, or their official
benevolence, or their protection, or the cushy
state jobs which they can guarantee us, if we
will place our resentment at their service.
Needless to say, I have assumed too much.
We *are* interested, aren't we? Let's not use
that nasty word, prostitution, though.
The situation is already depressing enough
without self-disparagement. . . .

In any case, as we "wait" we must make sure they do not, once again, convince us that it is "they" we have been waiting for.

A second thought. Before we try to decide what we are waiting for, let us make sure whether or not we are *waiting*. Perhaps, indeed, we have already given up hope of anything else. Perhaps we are unconsciously very busy in preparing the way for something which, in our right mind, we would be the last to wait for. In that case, not only are we not waiting for salvation, we are actively preparing our own destruction.

This leads to a third question. Forgive me for asking: but do we not, after all, *prefer* to be frustrated and led into despair? Are we not content to make despair a comfortable evasion — since it has certain elements of the picturesque — and by despair do we not come to terms with the meaninglessness of our own existence? Despair indeed seems very respectable, until one remembers that this is only the preparation to accept "their" next formula, which will explain, and exploit, our emptiness.

For you see, our emptiness is not innocent, not simply neutral, not "nothing." Our self-hatred is anything but contrition. It is the terrible spiritual vacuum into which malevolence can, like lightning, introduce itself in order to produce a universal explosion of hatred and destruction. This explosion is made possible by *our* emptiness. Without us, the emptiness of all the others would never be activated, and the death that sleeps in them would never be able to leap out and smash everything in sight.

And that reminds me of another thing: When we "stand by" we try to think of ourselves as independent, as standing on our own feet. It is true that as intellectuals we ought to stand on our own feet — but one cannot learn to do this until he has first recognized to what an extent he requires the support of the others. And it is our business to support one another against "them," not to be supported by "them" and used to crush "the others."

"They," of course, have never really been in any position to support anyone. "They" need us, but not our strength. They do not want us strong, but weak. It is our emptiness "they" need, as a justification of their own emptiness. That is why their support comes always, and only, in the form of bribes. We are nourished in order that we may continue to sleep. We are paid to keep quiet, or to say things that do not disturb the unruffled surface of that emptiness from which, in due time, the spark and the blast must leap out and release, in all men, the grand explosion.

And now the last question. It is the one you will probably like least of all. But I must ask it. Do we have any choice left? Do we not have to march where all the others march, and shout as madly as they? Worse still: are we not the kind of bystanders whose very "innocence" makes them guilty, makes them the obvious target for arbitrary terror?

If that is the case, and if we are able dimly
to realize what it means, we shall almost
certainly fail to resist the last and most
degrading temptation: the temptation of
the innocent intellectual who rushes fran-
tically into collaboration with "them," lends
himself to every defilement, *certain* that he
is being prepared for destruction, and, in the
end, asking only to be defiled as often and as
sordidly as possible before the final annihila-
tion takes place.

It is this that I fear for both of us: the mad,
frantic insistence on getting rid even of our
innocence, as if any other guilt would be
more bearable, in such a world, than the
guilt of being innocent.

When all this has been said, and pondered
by us both, I think you would take it as bad
manners for me to offer an easy solution.
And I am hardly mad enough to try it. I love
you enough (the word "love" slipped out
by mistake) to spare your legitimate pride.
It is not for me to provide the same kind of

clear, sweeping program of action which is "their" great temptation and their delusion. The very difficulty of our position comes from the fact that every definite program is now a deception, every precise plan is a trap, every easy solution is intellectual suicide. And that is why we are caught on the horns of a dilemma: whether we "act" or not we are likely to be destroyed. There is a certain innocence in not having a solution. There is a certain innocence in a kind of despair: but only if in despair we find salvation. I mean, despair of this world and what is in it. Despair of men and of their plans, in order to hope for the impossible answer that lies beyond our earthly contradictions, and yet can burst into our world and solve them if only there are some who hope in spite of despair.

The true solutions are not those which we force upon life in accordance with our theories, but those which life itself provides for those who dispose themselves to receive

the truth. Consequently our task is to dissociate ourselves from all who have theories
which promise clear-cut and infallible solutions, and to mistrust all such theories, not in
a spirit of negativism and defeat, but rather
trusting life itself, and nature, and if you will
permit me, God above all. For since man has
decided to occupy the place of God he has
shown himself to be by far the blindest, and
cruelest, and pettiest and most ridiculous of
all the false gods. We can call ourselves innocent only if we refuse to forget this, and if
we also do everything we can to make others
realize it.

To illustrate what I mean, I will remind you
of an innocent and ancient story, of a King
and his new clothes.

You know it, of course. It has been referred
to somewhere in psychoanalytical literature.
Tailors deceived a king, telling him they
would weave him a wonderful suit which
would be invisible to any but good men.
They went through all the motions of fitting

64

him out in the invisible suit, and the king, as well as all his courtiers claimed to "see" and to admire the thing. In the end the naked king paraded out into the street where all the people were gathered to admire his suit of clothes, and all did admire it until a child dared to point out that the king was naked.

You will perhaps find that my thought has taken on a sentimental tinge. But since the times have become what they have become, I dare to blurt this out. Have you and I forgotten that our vocation, as innocent bystanders — and the very condition of our terrible innocence — is to do what the child did, and keep on saying the King is naked, at the cost of being condemned as criminals? Remember, the child in the tale was the only one innocent: and because of his innocence, the fault of the others was kept from being criminal, and was nothing worse than foolishness. If the child had not been there, they would all have been madmen, or criminals. It was the child's cry that saved them.

◆ ◆ 2

A Signed Confession of Crimes against the State

I am the kind of person who must sooner or later, inevitably, fill pages of blank paper with the confession of secret crimes against the state. Why not be prepared? There is no time like the present — and who, in such a present, can promise himself a future?

My very existence is an admission of guilt. Placed before a blank sheet of paper, any blank sheet of paper, I instinctively begin to set down the list of my latest crimes. What else can I do? The very thoughts of a person like me are crimes against the state. All I have to do is think: and immediately I become guilty. In spite of all my efforts to correct this lamentable tendency to subversiveness and intellectual sabotage, I cannot possibly get rid of it.

What is the good of confessing it again? But that is the least I can do, for, they tell me, everyone must love the state. And those who one way or another have never been able to muster up the slightest interest in the state, must now be made to show either love or hatred. One way or the other. If you don't love, hate. And if you hate, then you can turn your hatred into love by confessing it, and expiating it. If you are fool enough to love, why not go the whole way and immolate yourself with self-accusations? After all, no love of yours can ever be good enough for the state! Unfortunately, my love is lukewarm at best.

Here is a blank sheet of paper. No one is forcing me to do this. I am trying to do it out of "love" (meaning of course hatred). (I am trying to convince myself that I am sufficiently interested in the state to hate it.)

It is not easy, yet. For this reason I am sometimes tempted to leave the paper the way it
is and not write on it at all. Or simply to sign
it, and let them write on it later. But no.
Red-blooded patriotism will have none of
this. Let me confess my secret and subversive
desire not to accuse myself. I have but one
life and one reputation to lay down for the
Nation, the People, and the Party. So let's go.

I declare that everything that I am now about
to write will be either true or false, and I
confess that neither I nor the state care which,
so long as something is written. Everything
that is written, anywhere, or by anybody, is
a potential confession of crime against the
state. Including the official documents of the
state itself, the official histories, etc., etc.
Everything written down, whether defiant
or servile, whether partisan or indifferent,
turns in the end into a death warrant. I will
mix defiance and servility in the desired pro-
portions and my indifference will make me
the partisan of all oppositions.

68 I confess that I am sitting under a pine tree doing absolutely nothing. I have done nothing for one hour and firmly intend to continue to do nothing for an indefinite period. I have taken my shoes off. I confess that I have been listening to a mockingbird. Yes, I admit that it is a mockingbird. I hear him singing in those cedars, and I am very sorry. It is probably my fault. He is singing again. This kind of thing goes on all the time. Wherever I am, I find myself the center of reactionary plots like this one.

I confess furthermore that there is a tanager around here somewhere. I do not deny that I have been looking for the tanager and after five minutes I have seen him. I am the only person who has seen this particular tanager at this particular time, since there is nobody else around. I confess that there is nobody else around because I came here on purpose to get away from the state. I avow, in a frantic paroxysm of grief, that the state and I are much better off when we have nothing to do with each other. And I even confess that I (in contradistinction to the state) believe that this separation is not only desirable but even possible. Indeed it is, at least temporarily, an accomplished fact. I confess it. I confess it. The birds are singing again, and I confess it.

(You say that this is indeed horrible, but that it is not yet horrible enough. I am sorry, I cannot improve on the truth. That is a refinement I must leave to the state, which is perfectly equipped to do a very good job of it. I am just writing down what I have actually done, or rather what I have not done. That is usually it: I just *don't do* the things that they do on one side or the other. I am therefore probably worse than all the rest, since I am neither a partisan nor a traitor. The worst traitor is the one who simply takes no interest. That's me. Here I sit in the grass. I watch the clouds go by, and like it. Quisling. Trotsky. Judas.)

I admit that nothing has happened all afternoon, and that it continues to happen. It is true, I have got my feet in an anthill, by mistake. (Ah, now we are getting somewhere!!) I might as well confess it. There are ants on the paper as I write. They are determined to take over all the writing, but meanwhile the sun shines and I am here under the pine trees. While there is still time I confess that there are ants on the paper, and a fly in my ear. I do not try to deny that there is a fly in my ear and another on my sleeve. Honestly I don't care. I am sorry. I have no desire to get rid of them. If I had a grain of true patriotism those flies would make a difference. I beg the forgiveness of the state.

The sun? Yes, it is shining. I see it shine. I am in full agreement with the sunshine. I confess that I have been in sympathy all along with the sun shining, and have not paused for two seconds to consider that it shines on account of the state. I am shattered by the realization that I have never attributed the sunshine to its true cause, namely the state. Clearly I am not worthy to exist another minute. And yet

I go on shamelessly. I continue to exist. Pretty soon the ants will take over all the sunshine, but while there is still time I confess it: the sun is shining.

Signed...................................

(*Deposition of reliable witness:* He has come to the wood with his shoes in his hand, and with a book. He has sat with papers and a book. He has done no work, but stood and sat in the sun over and around an anthill, at the sound of a bird. The ants are on his hands and feet while he is lying down, standing up, walking about, running, and even running very fast. Yes, there are ants all over the sunshine, running very fast.)

◆ ◆ ◆ PART THREE

Herakleitos the Obscure

◆ ◆ ◆ 1

Herakleitos : A Study

ONE OF the most challenging, inscrutable and acute of philosophers is Herakleitos of Ephesus, the "dark" *skoteinos, tenebrosus*. He lived in the Ionian Greek city sacred to Artemis, where he flourished at the turn of the fifth century B.C., in the days of the Greek tyrants, and of the Persian wars. He was a contemporary of Pindar and Aeschylus and of the victorious fighters of Marathon, but unlike the poets who wrote and sang in the dawn of the Attic Golden age, Herakleitos was a tight-lipped and cynical pessimist who viewed with sardonic contempt the political fervor of his contemporaries.

He was one of those rare spirits whose prophetic insight enabled them to see far beyond the limited horizons of their society. The Ionian world was the world of Homer and of the Olympian gods. It was a world that believed in static and changeless order, and in the laws of mechanical necessity — basically materialistic. Against this Olympian formalism, against the ritualism and the rigidity of the conventional exterior cult, the static condition of a society that feared all that was not "ordinary," Herakleitos rose up **75** with the protest of the Dionysian mystic. He spoke for the mysterious, the unutterable, and the excellent. He spoke for the logos which was the true law of all being — not a static and rigid form, but a dynamic principle of harmony-in-conflict. This logos-principle was represented by Herakleitos under the symbolic form of fire. However, fire was not only a symbol for Herakleitos. Later philosophers have derided the intuition by which Herakleitos designated fire as the "primary substance" of the cosmos — but perhaps the experience of our time, in which atomic science has revealed the enormous burning energy that can be released from an atom of hydrogen, may prove Herakleitos to have been nearer the truth than was thought by Plato or Aristotle. However, the "fire" of Herakleitos is something more than material. It is spiritual and "divine." It is the key to the spiritual enigma of man. Our spiritual and mystical destiny is to "awaken" to the fire that is within us, and our happiness depends on the harmony-in-conflict that results from this awakening. Our vocation is a call to spiritual oneness in and with the logos. But this interior fulfillment is not to be attained by a false peace resulting from artificial compulsion — a static and changeless "state" imposed by force of will upon the dynamic, conflicting forces with us. True peace is the "hidden attunement of opposite tensions" — a paradox and a mystery transcending both sense and will, like the ecstasy of the mystic.

Herakleitos left no writings of his own. Legend says that he composed a book which he presented to Artemis in her temple, but almost all the stories told of his life and exploits are to be mistrusted. It is much more likely that he wrote nothing at all. His sayings, those cryptic fragments which have so tenaciously survived, have come down to us in the writings of others. Herakleitos is quoted first of all by Plato and Aristotle, but also by later writers like Plotinus, Porphyry, Theophrastus, Philo, and several Christian Fathers such as Clement of Alexandria, Origen and Hyppolitus. Sometimes these philosophers and theologians quote Herakleitos with approval to illustrate a point of their own; more often they bring him up only in order to refute him. But St. Justin Martyr refers to him, along with Socrates, as a "Saint" of pre-Christian paganism. The fact that he is unknown to us except in the context which others have foisted on him makes him even more difficult to understand than he is in himself. Though the fragments which form his whole surviving work can be printed on two or three pages, long and laborious research is needed to untangle their authentic meaning and to liberate the obscure Ionian from the bias imposed on his thought by the interpretation of opponents.

His enigmatic sayings are terse paradoxes, often wearing the sardonic and oracular expression of the Zen *mondo*. The comparison suggests itself quite naturally in our day when Oriental thought has once again found a hearing (perhaps not always an intelligent hearing) in the West. Herakleitos appears at first sight to be more Oriental than Greek, though this appearance can easily be exaggerated, and Herakleitos himself warns us against irresponsible guesses in difficult matters. "Let us not conjecture at random about the greatest things." But it is true that the logos of Herakleitos seems to have much in common with the Tao of Lao-tse as well as with the Word of St. John. His insistence that apparently conflicting opposites are, at bottom, really one is also a familiar theme in Oriental thought. Herakleitos, we must remember, comes *before* Aristotle's principle of identity and contradiction. He does not look at things with the eyes of Aristotelian logic, and consequently he can say that opposites can be, from a certain point of view, the same.

The variations and oppositions between conflicting forces in the world are immediately evident to sense, and are not a complete illusion. But when men become too intent on analyzing and judging these oppositions, and separating them out into good and evil, desirable and undesirable, profitable and useless, they become more and more immersed in illusion and their view of reality is perverted. They can no longer see the deep, underlying connection of opposites, because they are obsessed with their superficial separateness. In reality, the distinction to be made is not between this force which is good and true, as against that force which is evil and false. Rather it is the perception of underlying oneness that is the key to truth and goodness, while the attachment to superficial separateness leads to falsity and moral error. This is why Herakleitos says, "to God all things are good and just and right, but men hold some things wrong and some right." God sees all things as good and right, not in their separateness by which they are in contrast to everything else, but in their inner harmony with their apparent opposites. But men separate what God has united.

Herakleitos looks on the world not as an abstractionist, but from the viewpoint of experience. However, and this is important, experience for Herakleitos is not merely the uninterpreted datum of sense. His philosophical viewpoint is that of a mystic whose intuition cuts through apparent multiplicity to grasp underlying reality as *one*. This vision of unity which Parmenides was to sum up in the universal concept of being was seen by the poet and mystic, Herakleitos, as "Fire."

We must be very careful not to interpret Herakleitos in a material way. Fire for him is a dynamic, spiritual principle. It is a divine energy, the manifestation of God, the power of God. God, indeed, is for Herakleitos "all things." But this is probably a much more subtle statement than we might be inclined to imagine at first sight, for he says that just as fire when it burns different kinds of aromatical spices becomes a variety of perfumes, so God working in the infinite variety of beings manifests Himself in countless appearances. God, strictly speaking, is then not merely "fire" or "earth" or the other elements, or all of them put together. His energy works, shows itself and hides in nature. He Himself is the Logos, the Wisdom, not so much "at work" in nature but rather "at play" there. In one of the fragments the "dark one" speaks of the logos in the same terms as the sapiential literature of the Bible speaks of the divine Wisdom: as a "child playing in the world":

When he prepared the heavens, I was present: when
   with a certain law and compass he enclosed the
   depths:
When he established the sky above, and poised the
   fountains of waters:
When he compassed the sea with its bounds, and set
   a law to the waters that they should not pass their
   limits:
When he balanced the foundations of the earth;
I was with him forming all things: and was delighted
   every day, playing before him at all times;
Playing in the world: and my delights were to be with
   the children of men.

— Proverbs 8:27-31

Herakleitos says: "Time is a child playing draughts. The kingly power is a child's." The reference to the game of draughts is a metaphor for his basic concept that all cosmic things are in a state of becoming and change, and this constant interplay of elements in a state of dynamic flux is the expression of the divine Law, the "justice," "hidden harmony" or "unity" which constantly keeps everything in balance in the midst of conflict and movement.

Wisdom, for Herakleitos, does not consist in that "polymathy" — the "learning of many things" — the scientific research which observes and tabulates an almost infinite number of phenomena. Nor does it consist in the willful, and arbitrary selection of one of many conflicting principles, in order to elevate it above its opposite and to place it in a position of definitive and final superiority. True wisdom must seize upon the very movement itself, and pene-

80

trate to the logos or thought within that dynamic harmony. "Wisdom is one thing — it is to know the thought by which all things are steered through all things." We are reminded of the words of the Old Testament Book of Wisdom — the one most influenced by Hellenic thought.

> And all such things as are hid and not foreseen, I have learned: for wisdom, which is the worker of all things, taught me.
> For in her is the spirit of understanding: holy, one, manifold, subtile, eloquent, active, undefiled, sure, sweet, loving that which is good, quick, which nothing hindereth, beneficient,
> Gentle, kind, steadfast, assured, secure, having all power, overseeing all things, and containing all spirits, intelligible, pure, subtile.
> For wisdom is more active than all active things: and reacheth everywhere by reason of her purity.
> For she is a vapour of the power of God, and a certain pure emanation of the glory of the almighty God: and therefore no defiled thing cometh into her.
> For she is the brightness of eternal light, and the unspotted mirror of God's majesty, and the image of his goodness.
> —Wisdom 7:21-26

Here in the inspired language of the sacred writer we find the Scriptural development which perfects and completes the fragmentary intuitions of Herakleitos, elevating them to the sublime level of contemplative theology and inserting them in the economy of those great truths of which Herakleitos could not have dreamt: the Incarnation of the Logos and man's Redemption and Divinization as the supreme manifestation of wisdom and of the "attunement of conflicting opposites."

The heart of Herakleitean epistemology is an implicit contrast between man's wisdom, which fails to grasp the concrete reality of unity-in-multiplicity and harmony-in-conflict, but which instead seizes upon one or other of the conflicting elements and tries to build on this a static and one-sided truth which cannot help but be an artificial fiction. The wisdom of man cannot follow the divine wisdom "one and manifold" in its infinitely varied movement. Yet it aspires to a universal grasp of all reality. In order to "see" our minds seize upon the movement around them and within them, and reduce it to immobility. If it were possible for them to fulfill their deepest wish, our minds would in fact impose on the dynamism of the cosmos a paralysis willed by our own compulsiveness and prejudice: and this would ruin the world. For if things were the way we would have them be, in our arbitrary and shortsighted conception of "order," they would all move in one direction toward their ruin, which would be the supreme disorder. All order based purely on man's conception of reality is merely partial — and partial order leads to chaos. Then all things would be consumed by fire — or by water. The real order of the cosmos is an apparent disorder, the "conflict" of opposites which is in fact a stable and dynamic harmony. The wisdom of man is the product of willfulness, blindness, and caprice and is only the manifestation of his own insensibility to what is right before his eyes. But the eyes and ears tell us nothing if our minds are not capable of interpreting their data.

And so Herakleitos, wielding the sharp weapon of paradox without mercy, seeks to awaken the mind of his disciple to a reality that is right before his eyes but that he is incapable of seeing. He wants to liberate him from the cult of "vanity" and to draw him forth from the sleep of formalism and subjective prejudices. Hence the paradox that Herakleitos, who is an uncompromising aristocrat and individualist in thought as well as in life, maintains that the truth is what is common to all. It is the "fire" which is the life of the cosmos as well as of each man. It is spirit and logos. It is "what is right before your eyes." But each individual loses contact with the One Fire and falls back into the "coldness" and moisture and "sleep" of his little subjective world. The awakening is then a recall from the sleep of individualism in this narrow, infantile sense, to the "common" vision of what is universally true. Unfortunately, the sleep of the individual spreads through society and is encouraged by social life itself when it is lived at a low level of spiritual intensity. The life and thought of the "many" is a conspiracy of sleep, a refusal to struggle for the excellence of wisdom which is hard to find. The "many" are content with the inertia of what is commonplace, "given" and familiar. They do not want anything new: or if they do, it must be a mere novelty, a diversion that confirms them in their comfortable inertia and keeps them from being bored with themselves, no more.

Hence, the "many" are complacently willing to be de-

luded by "polymathy" — the "learning of many things" —
the constant succession of novel "truths," new opinions,
new doctrines and interpretations, fresh observations and
tabulations of phenomena. This multiplicity beguiles the
popular mind with a vain appearance of wisdom. But in
reality it is nothing but intellectual and spiritual "sleep"
which deadens all capacity for the flash of mighty intuition
by which multiplicity is suddenly comprehended as basically one — penetrated through and through by the logos,
the divine fire.

The wise man must make tremendous efforts to grasp
"the unexpected": that is to say he must keep himself alert,
he must constantly "seek for himself" and he must not fear
to strive for the excellence that will make him an object of
hatred and mistrust in the eyes of the conventional majority — as did Hermodorus, whom the Ephesians threw out
of their city on the ground that if he wanted to excel he had
better go and do it somewhere else, for "we will have none
who is best among us."

The aristocratic contempt of Herakleitos for the conventional verbalizing of his fellow citizens was something
other than a pose, or a mad reflex of wounded sensibility.
It was a prophetic manifestation of intransigent honesty.
He refused to hold his peace and spoke out with angry concern for truth. He who had seen "the One" was no longer
permitted to doubt, to hedge, to compromise and to flatter.
To treat his intuition as one among many opinions would
have been inexcusable. False humility was an infidelity to
his deepest self and a betrayal of the fundamental insights

of his life. It would have been above all a betrayal of those whom he could not effectively contact except by the shock of paradox. Herakleitos took the same stand as Isaias, who was commanded by God to "blind the eyes of this people" by speaking to them in words that were too simple, too direct, too uncompromising to be acceptable. It is not given to men of compromise to understand parables, for as Herakleitos remarked: "When the things that are right in front of them are pointed out to them, they do not pay attention, though they think they do."

This is the tragedy which most concerns Herakleitos — and which should concern us even more than it did him: the fact that the majority of men think they see, and do not. They believe they listen, but they do not hear. They are "absent when present" because in the act of seeing and hearing they substitute the clichés of familiar prejudice for the new and unexpected truth that is being offered to them. They complacently imagine they are receiving a new light, but in the very moment of apprehension they renew their obsession with the old darkness, which is so familiar that it, and it alone, appears to them to be light.

Divinely impatient with the word-play and imposture of those pseudo-wise men who deceive others by collecting and reshuffling the current opinions, presenting old errors in new disguises, Herakleitos refused to play their pitiable game. Inspired, as Plato said, by the "more severe muses," he sought excellence, in his intuitions, at the cost of verbal clarity. He would go deep, and emerge to express his vision in oracular verses, rather than flatter the crowd by giving it what it demanded and expected of a philosopher, of a professional scholar we would say today. He would be like "the Lord at Delphi who neither utters nor hides his meaning but shows it by a sign." His words would be neither expositions of doctrine or explanations of mystery, but simply pointers, plunging toward the heart of reality: "fingers pointing at the moon." He knew very well that many would mistake the finger for the moon, but that was inevitable and he did not attempt to do anything about it.

It is interesting to compare Herakleitos with the Prometheus of Aeschylus. In Prometheus, the Firebearer, we see a similar revolt against Olympian formalism. We notice that the Titan, Prometheus, represents the older, more primitive, more "Dionysian" earth gods of archaic Greece, in rebellion against the newly established tyranny of Zeus. Aeschylus was consciously introducing politics into his tragedy, and as a result it strikes the modern reader with a tremendous force. The play is as actual as *Darkness at Noon* and the pressure to conform, exercised upon the chained Titan by Hermes, the agent of Zeus, has a shockingly totalitarian ring about it. A great crux for all interpreters of the Prometheus of Aeschylus, in this context, is whether his fire symbolizes science or wisdom. One might argue the point at length but in the end the only satisfactory solution is that it symbolizes both. For Prometheus, fire is science perfected by wisdom and integrally united with wisdom in a "hidden harmony." For the Olympians it is perhaps true to say that wisdom is not important, and that what they begrudge men is science, because science means power. Our interpretation of Prometheus will be completely perverse if we believe that what he wants is power. On the contrary, he represents the protest of love (which unites gods and men in a single family) against power (by which the gods oppress men and keep them in subjection). In this way Herakleitos rebelled against the accepted Olympian order of things preached by Homer and Hesiod.

As a result, most people found him terribly disturbing. They were "fools who are fluttered by every word," "dogs barking at everyone they do not know." In the end they had their revenge: the revenge that popular mediocrity takes upon singular excellence. They created a legend about Herakleitos — a legend which they could understand, for it consigned him forever to a familiar category and left them in comfort. They dismissed him as a crank, a misanthrope, an eccentic kind of beat who thought he was too good for them and who, as a result, condemned himself to a miserable isolation. He preferred loneliness to the warm security of their collective illusion. They called him "the weeping philosopher," though there is very little evidence of tears in his philosophy. The story developed that he finally retired from Ephesus in disgust and went to live alone in the mountains, "feeding on grass and plants." A writer referred to him as the "crowing, mob-reviling, riddling Herakleitos."

The implication was of course that Herakleitos was proud, that he despised the mob. Certainly contempt for other men is not compatible with humility in so far as it excludes love and empathy. It is altogether possible that Herakleitos was a proud man. But can we be sure of this? Is pride synonymous with an aristocratic insistence upon excellence? It takes humility to confront the prejudice and the contempt of all, in order to cling to an unpopular truth. In the popular mind, any failure to "conform," any aspiration to be different, is labeled as pride. But was Herakleitos exalting himself, his own opinions, or the common truth which transcends individuals and opinions? If we understand his doctrine we will see that this latter was the case.

A biographer (writing eight hundred years after his death), collected every story that might make Herakleitos look like a proud eccentric. Basing himself on the fact that Herakleitos had apparently been a member of the hereditary ruling family of Ephesus and had renounced his responsibilities, Diogenes Laertius recorded that:

> When he was asked by the Ephesians to establish laws he refused to do so because the city was already in the grip of its evil constitution. He used to retire to the temple of Artemis (outside the city) and play at knuckle bones with the children; when the Ephesians stood around him he said: "Why, villains, do you marvel? Is it not better to do this than join you in politics?"

No doubt this story is all that the popular mind was able to retain of his mysterious *logion* about "time being a child, playing draughts." They had taken the finger for the moon, and wanted history to ratify their error.

This story of Herakleitos playing knuckle bones in the temple is completely misleading. Several of his fragments show that he was deeply concerned with man's political life. But, as usual with him, the concern is far below the surface of trivial demagoguery and charlatanism which sometimes passes for "politics." Political life, for Herakleitos, was based on the common understanding of the wise, that is of those who were awake, who were aware of the logos, who were attuned to the inner harmony underlying conflicting opposites. Such men would not be easily deluded by the political passion excited by violence and partisan interest. They would not be swept away by popular prejudices or fears, for they would be able to see beyond the limited horizons of their own petty group. Political life is, substantially, the union of those minds who stand far above their group and their time, and who have a deeper, more universal view of history and of men. Such men are necessarily a minority. Their union is not achieved merely by a speculative participation in philosophical insights. It demands great moral energy and sacrifice. They must not be content to see the logos, they must cling to their vision, and defend their insight into unity with their very lives. "Those who speak with understanding must hold fast to what is common as a city holds fast to its law, and even more strongly."

Herakleitos is certainly not antisocial, certainly not an anarchist. He does not reject all law. On the contrary, wise and objective laws are the reflection of the hidden logos and accord with the hidden harmony underlying the seemingly confused movement on the surface of political life. Hence the function of law is not to impose an abstract arbitrary justice which is nothing but the willfulness of a tyrant guided only by his own fantasy and ambition. Law is an expression of that "justice" which is the living harmony of opposites. It is not the vindication of one part of reality as "good" in opposition to another part considered as "evil." It is the expression of the true good which is the inner unity of life itself, the logos which is common to all. Hence it defends the good of all against usurpation by particular groups and individuals seeking only their own limited advantage under the guise of universal "good."

Because of his aphoristic statements about "war" being the "father of all," Herakleitos has been referred to as a Fascist. The term is ridiculous, since by war he means chiefly the conflict of apparent opposites wherever it may be found, not simply military conflict. One might just as well call him a Marxist because this reconciliation of opposites looks like Hegelian dialectic. In point of fact, Herakleitos holds that political life is both absurd and unjust as long as the more excellent minds are excluded from fruitful participation in political life by the preponderance of mediocrities. Not that the world must be ruled by academic philosophers: but that the leadership must be in the hands of those who, by their well developed political and moral abilities, are able to discern the common justice, the logos, which is the true good of all and which, in fact, is the key to the meaning of life and of history.

Why write of Herakleitos in our day? Not, after twenty-five hundred years, to make him what he cannot be: popular. But he speaks to our age — if only some of us can hear him — he speaks in parables to those of us who are afraid of excellence in thought, in life, in spirit and in intellect. His message to us is spiritual, but few will accept it as such: for we have, by now, got far beyond an Ionian pagan. Or have we? Can it be that some of us who are Christians implicitly use our "faith" as an excuse for not going half as far as Herakleitos went? His thought demands effort, integrity, struggle, sacrifice. It is incompatible with the complacent security which can become for us the first essential in thought and life — we call it "peace." But perhaps Herakleitos is closer than we are to the spiritual and intellectual climate of the Gospel in which the Word that enlightens every man coming into the world is made flesh, enters the darkness which receives Him not: where one must be born again without re-entering the womb; where the Spirit is as the wind, blowing where it pleases, while we do not know where it comes from or where it is going. There was another, far greater than Herakleitos, who spoke in parables. He came to cast fire on the earth. Was He perhaps akin to the Fire of which Herakleitos spoke? The easy way to deny it is to dismiss the Ionian as a pantheist. Tag him with a philosophical label and file him away where he won't make anybody uncomfortable!

But not all Christians have done this. Gerard Manley Hopkins, whose vision of the world is Heraklitean as well as Christian, has wrestled with the thought in a poem that is no complacent evasion of the challenge. For Hopkins, the Cosmos is indeed a "Heraklitean fire." His concept of *inscape* is both Heraklitean and Scotistic. It is an intuition of the patterns and harmonies, the "living character" impressed by life itself revealing the wisdom of the Living God in the mystery of interplaying movements and changes. *"Million fueléd, nature's bonfire burns on."* The most special, *"clearest-selvéd"* spark of the divine fire is man himself. This spark is put out by death. But is death the end? Does the fire merely burn with another flame? Hopkins reaches further into the mystery, not playing with words but wrestling with the angel of tribulation, to reach the Resurrection when *"world's wildfire leaves but ash"* and *"I am all at once what Christ is . . . immortal diamond."*

Herakleitos did not know Christ. He could not know that the logos would be made flesh and dwell amongst us. Yet he had some intimation of immortality and of resurrection. Some of his mysterious sayings suggest New Testament texts about the Risen Life of man in Christ: "Man kindles for himself a light in the night time when he has died but is alive . . . he that is awake lights up from sleeping." True, he is talking only of the spiritual and intellectual awakening which is the experience of the enlightened one, discovering the logos. But the mystical quality of this experience makes it also a figure of resurrection and new life, in which Herakleitos evidently believed.

He spoke, as we saw above, of the wise man clinging with all his strength to the "common" thought which unites him with other enlightened minds. The wise man must cling to the logos and to his unity with those who are aware of the logos. He must bear witness to the "common" thought even at the cost of his own life. To die for the truth is then the "greatest death" and wins a "greater portion." What is this portion? "There awaits men when they die such things as they look not for nor dream of." The death of the wise man is the "death of fire"; a passage from darkness into greater light, from confusion into unity. The death of the fool clinging to subjective opinion and self-interest is the "death of earth or water," a sinking into coldness, darkness, oblivion and nonentity. Those who die the death of fire — the death which Christianity was to call martyrdom, and which Herakleitos definitely believed was a "witness" to the Fire and the Logos — become superior beings. They live forever. They take their place among the company of those who watch over the destinies of the cosmos and of men, for they have, in their lives, entered into the secret of the logos. "They who die great deaths rise up to become the wakeful guardians of the living and the dead." The aristocracy in which Herakleitos believed was then not an aristocracy of class, of power, of learning (all these are illusory). It is an aristocracy of the spirit, of wisdom: one might almost say of mysticism and of sanctity.

Note: The following version of some of the *Fragments* is compiled with considerable liberty. They are united with a definite purpose, I might say with a definite prejudice of my own as to their meaning. This implies that I have had the presumption to interpret

94

the "obscure one," by stringing his fragments together in such a way that they react upon one another and stimulate one another to give off lights that were perhaps not originally intended. I do not feel that I have betrayed the great Ionian, especially since I have followed such scholars as I felt I could trust most, above all F. M. Cornford who, to my mind, has understood the Pre-Socratics better than anyone else. The *Fragments* in their simple, dissociated form, may be found in John Burnet's *Early Greek Philosophy*, 4th ed. London and New York, 1945.

◆ ◆ ◆ 2

The Legacy of Herakleitos

I

I have sought for myself.

The things that can be seen, heard and learned are what I value.

It is wise to hearken not to me but to my Logos (Word), and to confess that all things are one.

Though this Logos is at all times true, yet men are as unable to understand it when they hear it for the first time, as before they have heard it at all. For although all things come to pass in accordance with this Word, men seem as if they had no experience of them, when they make trial of words and deeds.

95

96

Fools, when they do hear, are like the deaf: of them does the saying bear witness that they are absent when present.

Eyes and ears are false witnesses to men if they have souls that do not understand their language.

The many do not pay attention to what is right in front of their nose: and when these things are pointed out to them, they do not take note of them though they think they do.

They are estranged from that with which they are always in contact.

The waking have one common world, but the sleeping turn aside each into a world of his own.

It is not right to act and speak like men asleep.

If you do not expect the unexpected, you will not find it, for it is hard to be sought out, and difficult.

The fool is fluttered at every word.

The fool flutters every word.

II

The mysteries practiced among men are
   unholy mysteries . . .
. . . Night walkers, Magians, Bakchoi, Lenai
   and the initiated . . .
And they pray to images as though one were
   to talk to a man's house, knowing not
   what Gods or Heroes are!
They vainly purify themselves by defiling
   themselves with blood, just as if one who
   had stepped in the mud were to wash his
   feet in mud. Any man who marked him
   doing thus would think him out of his
   mind.

III

Nature loves to hide.
It rests by changing.

IV

The Lord whose is the oracle at Delphi
   neither utters nor hides his meaning, but
   shows it by a sign,

And the Sybil, with raving lips, uttering things mirthless without adornment and without scent reaches over a thousand years with her voice, thanks to the god in her.

V

Wisdom is one thing: it is to know the thought by which all things are steered through all things.

The wise is one only. He is willing and unwilling to be called by the Name of *Zen* (i.e. the living one — sometimes translated as Zeus).

VI

Time is a child playing draughts.
The kingly power is a child's.

VII

The learning of many things does not teach understanding, or else it would have taught Hesiod and Pythagoras.

Pythagoras, son of Mnesarches, practiced
    scientific inquiry beyond all other men,
    and picking here and there in their writ-
    ings, claimed for his own a wisdom that
    was nothing but a knowledge of many
    truths, and an imposture.
Hesiod is most men's teacher. Men are sure
    he knew very many things, a man who did
    not know day and night! They are one.

VIII

Homer was wrong in saying: "Would that
    conflict might perish from among gods
    and men." He did not see that he was
    praying for the destruction of the uni-
    verse; for if his prayer were heard, all
    things would pass away.
(Men do not know how what is at variance
    agrees with itself. It is a harmony of oppo-
    site tensions, like that of the bow and lyre.)

Every beast is driven to pasture with blows!

IX

100   Of all whose discourses I have heard,
           there is none who manages to discover
           that wisdom is apart from all.

X

The way of man has no wisdom,
   but the way of God has.

XI

All things are fire.

The cosmos, which is the same for all,
No one of the gods or men has made;
But it was ever, is now, and ever shall be
   an ever-living Fire
With measures of it flaming up
And other measures going out.

The transformations of Fire are, first of
   all sea;
And half of the sea is earth,
Half whirlwind.

All things are an exchange for Fire
And Fire for all things,
Even as goods for money,
And money for goods.

Fire is emptiness and fullness.

Fire in its advance will judge and convict all
    things:
How can one hide from that which never sets?

XII

God is day and night, winter and summer,
    conflict and peace, fullness and emptiness;
    but He takes various shapes, just as fire,
    when it is mingled with aromatic spices, is
    named according to the scent of each.

XIII

All things change.

The sun is new every day.

You cannot step twice into the same stream;
    for fresh waters are ever flowing upon you.

102 We must know that conflict is common to all, and strife is justice, and that all things come into being and pass away through strife.

The straight and crooked path of the fuller's comb is one and the same.

Asses would rather have straw than gold.
Oxen are happy when they find bitter weeds to eat.
To God all things are good and fair and right,
But men hold some things wrong, and some right.
Good and ill are one.

The way up and the way down are one and the same.
In the circumference of a circle the beginning and the end are one.

It is not good for men to get all they wish to get.

It is the opposite which is good for us.

XIV

Souls smell in hades.

XV

The hidden harmony is better than the open.

You will not find the boundaries of the soul
By traveling in any direction,
So deep is the measure of it.

Man kindles light for himself in the night
    time when he has died but is alive.
The sleeper whose vision has been put out
    lights up from the dead.
He that is awake
    lights up from sleeping.

XVI

It is hard to fight
    against one's heart's desire.
Whatever the desire wishes to get
    it buys at the soul's cost.

Unruly desire needs to be extinguished even
    more than a house on fire.

XVII

104

The wisest man is an ape compared to God
just as the most beautiful ape is ugly
compared to man.

XVIII

Dogs bark at everyone they do not know.

The Ephesians would do well to hang
themselves, every grown man of them,
and leave the city to beardless lads;
for they have cast out Hermodorus, the
best man among them, saying: "We will
have none who is best among us; if there
be any such, let him be so elsewhere and
among others!"

XIX

Those who speak with understanding must
hold fast to what is common as a city holds
fast to its law, and even more strongly. For
all human laws are fed by the one divine
law.

Thought is common to all.
So we must follow the common,
yet though my Logos is common the many
live as if they had a wisdom of their own.
They are estranged from that with which
   they are in constant contact.
The waking have one common world, but
   the sleeping turn aside each into a world
   of his own.

The most esteemed of them knows only
   illusions and clings to them
Yet certainly justice shall overtake the makers
   of lies and the false witnesses.

The people must fight for its law as for its
   walls.
Gods and men honor those who are slain in
   battle.

One is as ten thousand to me, if he be the
   best.
And it is law, too, to obey the counsel of one.

In Priene lived Bias, the son of Teutamas,
Who is of more account than the rest.

X X

106

There await men when they die
such things as they look not for,
   nor dream of!

Greater deaths
win greater portions. . . .

. . . They (who die great deaths)
rise up and become the wakeful guardians
of the living and the dead.